CONTENTS

THE MATERIAL IN THIS GUIDE

HELP FOR *FIND YOUR FIT* LEADERS................. 5
get ready for discovery

SESSION ONE: UNWRAPPING YOU 8
explain what you're going to do

SESSION TWO: TALENTS.............................10
discern what God made you good at

SESSION THREE: SPIRITUAL GIFTS 12
unlock God's big-purpose gifts

SESSION FOUR: PERSONALITY TYPE 14
figure out where you fit best

SESSION FIVE: VALUES 16
decide between good, better, and best things

SESSION SIX: PASSIONS 18
commit yourself to the causes you care about most

REPRODUCIBLE MASTERS 20

HELP FOR FIND YOUR FIT LEADERS
GET READY FOR DISCOVERY

The youth book *Find Your Fit* highlights how God has wisely and wildly gifted youth in five areas—talents, spiritual gifts, personality, values, and passions. *Find Your Fit* is an organized approach to help youth discover how all those gifts add up to who they are, why they're here on planet earth, and what they do best. And it shows youth how their giftedness can radically impact how they live daily for God.

Find Your Fit was designed for youth to study solo. After all, no one but an individual holding the book can decide to take the task of "finding himself" seriously. No one can pry into a young person's mind and tell her exactly how to answer the questions and exercises. And no one can predict what a youth might discover about his God-given uniqueness. In other words, *Find Your Fit* requires the personal honesty and investment of each reader.

But a student's study of *Find Your Fit* can be GREATLY enriched by the coaching of a caring adult and interaction with peers.

USING *FIND YOUR FIT* WITH GROUPS

A group of students can encounter life-changing discoveries by simply reading *Find Your Fit* and asking together, "So what did you figure out about yourself? And what's God got to do with it?" The sessions below, though, assume that an adult or older youth is leading a group through a more structured *Find Your Fit* experience. You can teach each piece of the book individually. Or you can teach through the book in one of two formats: a full-blown six sessions or an abbreviated three sessions. The first format could easily become the basis of a series of youth meetings or of a week-long camp; the latter format can be the backbone of a weekend retreat.

BEEFING UP YOUR BACKGROUND

Adult leaders of *Find Your Fit* will likely see themselves in the book's pages and enter into their own process of discovering their unique giftedness. However, they also benefit greatly from reading *LifeKeys*, the adult book by Jane Kise, David Stark, and Sandra Hirsh upon which *Find Your Fit* is based. There are also additional training resources based on the adult book. A leader's guide at the back of *LifeKeys* expands on some of the ideas offered here, and the *LifeKeys Leadership Resource* (US$60), available directly from Bethany House Publishers at (800) 829-2503, is a two-inch binder containing handouts, overhead masters, teaching notes, and material. Although it is styled for adult groups, it still provides background and material useful for teaching older youth.

BEFORE YOU START

Find Your Fit succeeds best when its leaders prepare well for leading—and then let students' own discovery and discussion run wild. Some hints for getting the most out of *Find Your Fit*:

- **Bring a caring attitude.** *Find Your Fit* uncovers

this-is-how-I'm-made-and-no-one-had-better-laugh-at-me kinds of issues. It surfaces new feelings about self and is used by God in many different ways. It's big, highly personal material. So it's important to create an encouraging atmosphere when you lead participants through *Find Your Fit*. Aim for *safety to share* and *an absolute ban on slams*. Prepare anyone who helps you to pray for youth who will look hard at how God has wired them.

- **Choose a format.** Tailor how you use *Find Your Fit* to meet the specific needs of your group.

    A Piece or Two: You can take newcomers to your group through *talents* as a "welcome to how God made you" or as a basic way to match youth to service opportunities. You can take student leaders through *spiritual gifts*, helping them see ways to minister that fit their gifts. You can give families fresh understanding of one another through *personality types* and *values*. You can use *talents* and *personality types* to build teamwork by showing how each team member functions best. And the *passions* chapter can charge up students to change the world.

    The biggest value of Find Your Fit, *however, is giving your youth multiple mirrors to examine themselves. It's designed to be the best-rounded self-discovery series available*—highlighting not just talents or spiritual gifts but also personality type, values, and passions. Two options work best:

    Six Sessions: Follow this guide to offer one session a week. Spreading *Find Your Fit* over six sessions gives students time to think through the material and process what they learn. Six sessions would also let you do *Find Your Fit* one piece a day at a one-week camp.

    Three Sessions: Use sessions two, three, and four of this guide to help your students through the chapters on talents, spiritual gifts, and personality type. Students can work through the crucial remaining chapters on values and passions on their own. Three sessions let you cover the core of *Find Your Fit* on a two-day retreat.

    If you use the three-session option, you will also want to look over session one for ways to introduce *Find Your Fit*.

- **Decide how much homework you want to give.** Especially if you decide to use an abbreviated format, don't be shy about assigning material to be read and worked through before your class. Most youth find the material both useful and engaging. Personal prereading is the best way to allow time for participants to ask questions, spend time in small-group discussions, and tie together what they have learned. *However,* if your group isn't in a pattern of prereading for your meetings, you can also introduce a topic in your session and encourage your students to follow up by reading the chapter on their own.

- **Don't rush individual sessions.** We suggest you allow each session 75 minutes, which provides time for teaching the topic, small-group discussion, and individual questions. If you run shorter sessions, have leaders available afterward to answer questions.

- **Don't rush the process.** The real work of *Find Your Fit* is the time students spend thinking between sessions and even after completing the book. Give your students permission to *not* decide immediately what their gifts are. Identifying giftedness in *Find Your Fit*'s five areas can be a long process for some students.

- **Set reasonable and flexible goals.** Give students freedom to take away different things from your sessions together—everything from ideas for volunteering, tips for getting along at home or school, a list of possible career areas, a sense of God's call on their lives, an acceptance of God's design of others, or simple thankfulness for their own gifts.

- **Determine group size.** Bigger groups give you a good mix of participants. Smaller groups offer more time to talk. Get the best of both by taking a bunch of students through *Find Your Fit* and breaking them into adult- or older youth-led small groups for discussion.

- **Know what you're teaching.** You could teach *Find Your Fit* by working through the chapters to stay one step ahead of students. You will do better, though, if you work through the whole book yourself first—not just to learn more about who *you* are, why *you* are here, and what *you* do best, but to make the material your own. You will also see how all of the five pieces of *Find Your Fit* complement one another. If you want a more straight-laced but still thoroughly engaging treatment of the same material, grab a copy of *LifeKeys*, the adult book on which *Find Your Fit* was based.

- **Get some help.** Recruit teaching assistants/small-group leaders from your congregation, organization, or community who have experience in human resources development. They might be teachers, school counselors, MBTI© practitioners, or others who have completed a process similar to *LifeKeys*. And as you graduate *Find Your Fit* participants, fold students back into the process as assistant small-group leaders for subsequent sessions. Volunteers benefit from taking the class again and get new insights from a second or even third pass through the materials.

- **Be sensitive to parent/child dynamics.** Some youth will enter the *Find Your Fit* group under a load of parental pressure—whether simply to get involved at church or to figure out their future. Read our letter to parents at the beginning of the book and help everyone think outside the box. It's normal for parents and children, for example, to have different personality types—and it's also easy for everyone to interpret those differences as rebellion. But don't paint parents as the bad guys; youth desperately need their input. Aim to make your *Find Your Fit* experience a safe place for students *and* for parents.
- **Give space.** Some youth work through *Find Your Fit* and feel like they've unearthed buried treasure. Others unwrap their gifts and wonder if God left them less-than-perfect Christmas presents. Whatever students figure out about themselves, it's deeply personal. If they don't feel like talking, don't force them into a touchy-feely processing session. For youth that can feel like the emotional equivalent of tying them up and dragging them across the room.

PUTTING IT TOGETHER

Each lesson has four main elements:

- **Get It Going.** An activity to help you jump-start your session.
- **Talk It Up.** Tips to talk through the key points of each chapter.
- **Work It Out.** Small group exercises to identify and discuss each person's gifts.
- **Wrap It Up.** Ideas for putting what you've learned to use.

REMEMBER GOD

Find Your Fit is rooted in serious research and much astute biblical insight. It's deep. It's life-changing. It's also supposed to be fun. Let *Find Your Fit* prompt you and your group to humble celebration of your gifts and promote thundering applause for God's graciousness. God is the one behind all of our gifts:

> *For you [God] created my inmost being; you knit me together in my mother's womb. I praise you because I am fearfully and wonderfully made; your works are wonderful, I know that full well* (Psalm 139:13–14).
>
> *Every good and perfect gift is from above, coming down from the Father of the heavenly lights, who does not change like shifting shadows* (James 1:17).

CONTACTING US

We want to hear from you! Let us know how you and your group use *Find Your Fit* and what you discover. You can contact us (Jane Kise and Kevin Johnson) at

Bethany House Publishers
11400 Hampshire Ave. S.
Minneapolis, MN 55438

Or (so much faster) at

kevin@thewave.org

SESSION ONE
UNWRAPPING YOU

EXPLAIN WHAT YOU'RE GOING TO DO

You will likely want one session to set up what your *Find Your Fit* sessions are all about. In a group where students don't know one another well, take time to get acquainted in this session before bigger, deeper discussions hit later. Even in a group where everyone is a familiar face, take time to dive into new-but-non-threatening facts about yourselves.

GET IT GOING

In a starter session, any crowd breaker will do to get your group interacting. But don't just get your group *moving*—get your group primed to *talk* with these or similar questions. Many participants won't come busting to share deeply, so start with facts that people can share at whatever level they find comfortable. List (at most) three of the following questions on a whiteboard or overhead, allowing each participant to choose one or two they prefer to discuss. Break into small groups if necessary.

- What were your parents thinking when they gave you your name—first or middle? What's the history/heritage of your last name?
- Did you have a nickname growing up? How did you get that name? What did/do you think about it?
- Would you rather have a different name? Have you ever gone into a situation where no one knew you—and fibbed and told someone your name was different? What happened?
- When you were little, what did you want to be when you grew up? Have you stuck to that dream? If not, what changed your mind?
- If you had to pick one thing that's been THE highlight of your life, what would it be? What made it so great?

TALK IT UP

You'll want to next offer some general instructions for how you'll run your *Find Your Fit* sessions:

- The schedule and exercises assume your youth have preread the assigned chapters and completed the exercises in advance.
- Instruct students to set aside about an hour per week to read the materials and complete the exercises. That will help them benefit the most from the next session.
- Tell how participants can keep on track if they miss a session.
- Students may want help as they work through *Find Your Fit*. Can they get help outside of class?

Use chapter 1 to prepare a talk introducing *Find Your Fit* and what you hope your youth will learn. Whether your talks are formal or casual, aim at these topics:

- How do we feel squeezed—forced to conform in unhealthy ways and to hide who we really are?
- Who tells us whether we are gifted—or not?
- What does God have to do with how you're made? You can use REPRODUCIBLE MASTER 1—PSALM 139:14 to highlight the wonder of God's workmanship.
- How might God help us "find ourselves"? Use RE-

PRODUCIBLE MASTER 2—FIND YOUR FIT to help you explain the process. Why is each area important?

- What will keep us from succeeding in what we study?

Lastly, talk about some class "rules of operation":

- Things shared within the class are to be kept *confidential*.
- There are no *right* or *wrong answers* for much of this material.
- There's no such thing as a stupid question.
- You'll try to give equal time to each participant so a few people don't hog the discussion time.

WORK IT OUT

Make a class wish list. Ask the entire group for expectations they have for studying *Find Your Fit*—or discuss expectations in small groups, taking time to report back to the whole group. Take time for the process until all expectations have surfaced. Record what your youth want to learn on a flip chart or whiteboard so everyone can see them.

Be sure to keep a copy of the wish list so you and other leaders can use class time wisely and remind participants throughout your sessions what answers you're trying to dig up.

WRAP IT UP

Some closing remarks:

- Your *Find Your Fit* sessions are just a start. Most students will continue to work through what they have learned long after the last session.
- Participants vary in how they approach *Find Your Fit*. Some people whip through the exercises, some obsess over each answer, and others need encouragement to work hard.
- There are no ungifted people! The Bible promises us that. If students struggle with discovering how they are gifted, encourage them to come to you and/or other leaders for help.
- God made us for a reason. This class begins the process of discovering what we were created to do, the places or environments where we can best use our gifts, and the causes we feel passionate about.

Be sure to allow time for questions about the class.

NEXT SESSION

Have your students read *Find Your Fit* chapter 2—and do the exercises—to prep for your next session.

SESSION TWO
TALENTS
DISCERN WHAT GOD MADE YOU GOOD AT

Talents are easy to grasp—so they're a great place to start in helping students understand themselves. The *Find Your Fit* chapter "How to Locate a Life: Talents" is based on John Holland's theory of job choices and the Strong Interest Inventory™.

GET IT GOING

Here are a couple choices in introducing the six interest themes in *Find Your Fit*:

- **Magazine Sort.** To kick off class, place a pile of magazines on each of six tables—one set for each interest area. Allowing students to wander around and pick the mags they like best will be a good real-life indication of their biggest interests. After a time of wandering around, ask students to stand by their favorite table and explain why they prefer those magazines.

  Some suggested magazines: Realistic: *Popular Mechanics, Field & Stream, Runner, Gardening and Outdoor Living Ideas*. Investigative: *Discovery, Scientific American, PC Magazine, Astronomy, Chess Life*. Artistic: *Rolling Stone, Gourmet, Writers Digest, Design*. Social: *Psychology Today, People, Life, Entertainment Weekly*. Enterprising: *Money, New Republic, Leadership, Forbes, Harvard Business Review*. Conventional: *Consumer Digest, Reader's Digest, Popular Crosswords, Home Remodeling*.

- **Living Hexagon.** In this activity you will have participants self-select their top interest theme as they hear each theme described. In advance, make a poster for each of the interest areas and hang them in the room—a simple, big letter on a large piece of construction paper works well. Post your signs following the hexagon order (Realistic, Investigative, Artistic, Social, Enterprising, Conventional).

  Inform the group that they will be constructing a "Living Hexagon." Have everyone gather around the Realistic sign as you describe that area using the note card REPRODUCIBLE MASTER 3—REALISTIC TYPE. People who feel that description describes them can stay at that sign. Others move on as you describe the Investigative gift and so on around the hexagon of interest areas using REPRODUCIBLE MASTERS 3–5. Tell the participants that they can move to another interest area later if they feel that it describes them better. As you work through the descriptions, make sure you value each interest area. It's okay, for example, to easily keep your locker or bedroom clean. That's a gift.

  If you're working through *Find Your Fit* with one or just a few students, flip through the cartoons and descriptions together to get the same point.

  When you have finished describing each of the six themes, your students will be grouped in the areas most interesting to them. You can have them sit down in these groups for discussions of the talents found in their particular interest area—or return to their original places and regroup after your talk.

- **Movie Party.** If you are truly ambitious, you can assemble a series of movie clips to fit each interest area. For instructions see the teacher's guide for the *Find Your Fit Discovery Workbook*, available at *www.thewave.org/fit.htm* or through Changing Church for the cost of shipping (800)-874-2044.

TALK IT UP

Use chapter 2 to plan your talk on talents. Your goal is to explain the concept of talents or "life gifts" and to make the point that every individual has special interest patterns. Some main ideas:

- How do we know we have talents?
- What main characteristics describe each interest area?
- Is one interest area better than another?
- How do different talents help our group to function best?
- What good are these specific things called life gifts? Are they really gifts?
- What do life gifts have to do with jobs?

Allow time for questions.

WORK IT OUT

Regroup using the interest area groups formed above. Have each group discuss and then talk to the larger group about three questions:

- What pieces of the interest area description best fit us? (Have students refer to the description of their interest area, found on pages 35–52 of *Find Your Fit*.)
- How can our church or community use us right now? (Start with asking which life gifts the participants have used—at work, home, school, volunteering. If your students have completed prior to class the detailed "Life Gifts" chart for their interest area, have them share what they discovered. Otherwise, have them look at that page now.)
- What would we like the other groups to know about us? (Have each group develop a list to report to the other groups.)

Some other questions to consider: What makes you afraid to use your talents? When have you liked using your life gifts? When have you been jealous of other people's talents? What should you do if it doesn't seem you have a gift you want? What do practice and training have to do with your gifting?

Note: If you have LOTS of time or want to go deeper on a retreat with this subject, check out the additional suggestions and group exercises in the teacher's guide for the *Find Your Fit Discovery Workbook,* available at www.thewave.org/fit.htm.

WRAP IT UP

Cover the "So Where Do You Go From Here?" section (pages 57–59) as best fits your group. Encourage students who haven't worked through the Life Gifts section of their interest area to do that—and give all students a reason to work through the other Life Gifts charts: They are *highly* likely to find more of their gifts sprinkled through other areas.

NEXT SESSION

Have your youth read *Find Your Fit* chapter 3—and do the exercises—to prep for your next session.

SESSION THREE
SPIRITUAL GIFTS

UNLOCK GOD'S BIG-PURPOSE GIFTS

Even committed Christians vary widely on how much exposure they have had to the Bible's teachings on spiritual gifts. The approach of *Find Your Fit* to spiritual gifts is meant to help beginners—those who don't know enough about spiritual gifts to feel at ease with the idea or ready to spot their possible gifts.

Believe it or don't, that's most of us. Researcher George Barna says that only 31% of *adults* who have *heard* of spiritual gifts are able to *identify* even one that they possess. In settings that emphasize spiritual gifts our approach may seem basic, but the majority of Christians lack knowledge in this area.

GET IT GOING

Start your spiritual gifts session with this simple activity:

Spiritual Gifts Bingo. Make up a sheet of paper with squares to initial as students mingle and find others who have "Gone on a mission trip," "Taught Sunday school," "Sang in a church choir." Make the sheet fit your setting, and include ways your youth have used their spiritual gifts that aren't churchy: "Gave wise advice to a friend" or "Encouraged a neighbor." An example from one church is found in REPRODUCIBLE MASTER 6. Notice that the statements in this chart—goofy as they seem—fit specific spiritual gifts:

Column 1—Encouragement and Mercy
Column 2—Helps
Column 3—Leadership
Column 4—Evangelism
Column 5—Discernment
Column 6—Teaching

Process this activity by asking your students what they know about spiritual gifts: What are they? Where are they found in the Bible? Do they make you automatically holy? How do you know if you have them? These questions naturally transition into your talk.

TALK IT UP

Check out chapter 3 to prepare a talk introducing spiritual gifts. Your goal is to explain what spiritual gifts are and how they differ from talents. (Unlike life gifts, spiritual gifts are given especially to further God's spiritual purposes.)

Key points from the chapter:

- Why don't we know much about spiritual gifts?
- Why did God give spiritual gifts?
- How do we use spiritual gifts in real life?
- Which gifts does God like best? (trick question—He likes them all!)
- What do gifts have to do with spiritual maturity?

You will probably want to address details of specific gifts. REPRODUCIBLE MASTERS 7–16 give you succinct outlines of the ten spiritual gift groupings covered in *Find Your Fit*. Here's a helpful format to cover a lot of ground quickly:

- Read the name of the gift and its definition;
- Use the explanatory material in *Find Your Fit* or a brief, real-life illustration from your group or church of someone who has the gift;
- Note the possible signs someone has the gift;

- Share one tip from the book on how to develop that gift.

After you have explained a gift, ask for a *show of hands* from participants who believe they possess each gift. Raising a hand takes honesty and boldness—but it's a great chance to talk about how (a) humility is a realistic assessment of our gifts—no more, no less; and (b) acknowledging our gifts is a way of thanking God.

Note: If you are using the *Find Your Fit Discovery Workbook* rather than *Find Your Fit*, REPRODUCIBLE MASTERS 17–18 provide abbreviated scoring sheets for your youth to use as you teach spiritual gifts.

We *consistently* find ourselves short of time for this talk because of participants' great interest in the subject. Your whole next session is devoted to personality types, but you can shorten the exercises in session five (values) to allow more time for spiritual gifts. By that point, your youth will have had time to reread the descriptions and have probably identified their gifts. That's a good time to come back and answer further questions.

Big Hint: You'll want to be ready to address the differing theologies concerning gifts like speaking in tongues and healing. Many youth have questions about them. Make sure you're clear on the potential overlap among the gifts of knowledge, prophecy, discernment, and wisdom.

WORK IT OUT

Given the time you will likely need to teach through spiritual gifts, this small-group exercise is optional (but pretty productive). It can also be used at the start of this session in place of Spiritual Gifts Bingo:

Read to your students the following scenario. (The scenario is also REPRODUCIBLE MASTER 19—MY FRIEND MEGAN for use as an overhead transparency.) Have your students respond to the questions first *by themselves* and then *in a small group*.

Megan is a ninth-grade friend whose dad just died after a long battle with cancer. Besides Megan, her family includes a fourth grader, a second grader, and a preschooler. Megan's mom works three afternoons a week and has no close family in the area. Megan is angry that she has to care for the younger kids so much—not to mention the fact that she feels hurt over her dad's death. She's had to drop out of after-school activities because she can't find a ride home, and her grades are slipping.

- List a few of the needs Megan's family would have. Then individually choose the one you would be most interested in responding to and describe what you would do to help.
- Share your responses as a group. How do the various responses reflect your differing spiritual gifts? Your life gifts?

WRAP IT UP

If you have had time to do the optional small-group discussion, come back together as a large group and put all of the responses on a board. You can then summarize all the ways people with different spiritual gifts make God's work happen in the world.

Cover the "So Where Do You Go From Here?" section (pages 84–85) as best fits your group.

Encourage students who haven't completed the spiritual gifts inventories to look first at the gifts they think they might have—and all students to work through the rest of the spiritual gifts questions.

NEXT SESSION

Have your youth read *Find Your Fit* chapter 4—and do the exercises—to prep for your next session.

SESSION FOUR
PERSONALITY TYPE

FIGURE OUT WHERE YOU FIT BEST

Talents and spiritual gifts tell us what we're good at. The next step is to understand how and where we might best put those gifts to use. While personality type doesn't explain everything about people, it does do an excellent job of helping them understand themselves, appreciate others, know the work/volunteer setting best for them, and make sense of some of their biggest life choices. Personality type can be used for a stack of other purposes, but with the time available it's important to stick to using type *to guide your students to the places that are the most appealing to them.*

The chapter "Finding the Places You Fit: Personality Type" in *Find Your Fit* is based on the theory popularized by the Myers-Briggs Type Indicator© (MBTI©), the most widely used personality test in the world today.

GET IT GOING

Check out chapter 4 to prepare a talk introducing personality type. You can use REPRODUCIBLE MASTER 20 to help you cover key points:

- Personality type is based in *observable behavior*. It has nothing to do with wacko stuff like horoscopes or reading bumps on people's heads.
- Type describes natural preferences for how people *get energized, take in information, make decisions,* and *steer their lives*. In case anyone asks, Jesus was the one person who could effectively use all eight preferences. He wasn't any one type.
- Preferences influence the settings where people choose to put our talents and spiritual gifts to work. Understanding type gives insights into people and the work settings where they fit best, as well as insights into their relationships.
- Personality types are God-given. There are no "good" or "bad" types. Each has a unique contribution to make.
- Type is not an excuse. It helps people work on their weaknesses and learn to "step out of the box," to act outside their natural preferences. Everyone has a distinct personality type—mostly set before birth but subject to change by surroundings. By knowing their personality type, people can best utilize their strengths.
- You can also put thes key points on posters to take up and refer to throughout the session.

TALK IT UP

Here are two ways to introduce the topic of personality type:

- **"Forced Choice" Option 1:** Help your students catch the differences between personality preferences. Use the material on REPRODUCIBLE MASTERS 21–24 to teach through Extraversion vs. Introversion, Sensing vs. Intuition, Thinking vs. Feeling, and Judging vs. Perceiving. As you give the scoop on each pair, have students divide to each side of your classroom according to what fits them best (E's to one side, I's to the other—for example). Have students record their choices in their books.

  Note: This exercise doesn't contain the same detail as content in the book (and so it might not give as accurate an indication of type). Don't skip the "DON'T MISS THIS" summary that appears a few paragraphs below, after "Forced Choice" Option 2.

Another Note: This is a particularly easy spot for students to go with what they think is the "right" answer. Fifty percent of the U.S. population, for example, tests as introverted. Yet in a typical teen group eighty to ninety percent might claim to be extraverts. Emphasize the need to answer as honestly as possible.

And Yet Another Note: It's difficult for students under age 14 to discern their personality type. Your goal with younger students is to give them permission to be different. Concrete example: We aren't all wired to want to be with people all the time. It isn't necessarily wrong, for instance, to like to spend time alone just thinking.

- **"Forced Choice" Option 2:** Look at REPRODUCIBLE MASTERS 25–27 for a more involved forced choice exercise useful with older youth. The exercise is easier done than said, and it's a great way to get at the differences between personality types.

DON'T MISS THIS

After either exercise, use REPRODUCIBLE MASTERS 28–35 to quickly sum up the differences in preferences (E and I, S and N, T and F, J and P).

WORK IT OUT

For small-group discussion, have your youth sit with their type group—that is, in one of the sixteen types detailed in the book. If you have a small group or there are types with a single representative, ask that individual to be a group of one so that he or she can report to the rest of the group about the characteristics of that type.

Use the type descriptions on pages 110–141 to study and discuss how their type affects their lives. What do they learn about themselves in these descriptions? How could recognizing their type help them in school, work/service, or just getting along in life? What do they think of the "big picture" characteristics of their type given at the top of each type summary?

Let each group briefly report to the large group three things that they would most like the other types to know about them.

Caution: Class time is very short. Most MBTI© practitioners prefer three hours to introduce these concepts. If you administer the MBTI©, you may want to schedule additional time for this session.

Note: If you have LOTS of time or want to go deeper on a retreat with this subject, check out the additional suggestions and group exercises in the teacher's guide for the *Find Your Fit Discovery Workbook,* available free at www.thewave.org/fit.htm or through Changing Church for the mere cost of shipping (800-874-2044). You can also enrich your presentation by making overheads of the type cartoons in *Find Your Fit* and the adult *LifeKeys Leadership Resource.*

Another note: You can find highly useful details on the MBTI© in the *LifeKeys Leadership Resource* or in Gordon Lawrence's easy-to-understand and affordable "Descriptions of the 16 Types" pamphlet, available at 10 for $5 from CAPT (1-800-777-CAPT).

WRAP IT UP

Cover the "So Where Do You Go From Here?" section (pages 106–109) as best fits your group. Encourage students to study the pages that detail their personality type (110–141). Which descriptions pat them on the back? Which statements point out personal characteristics they should work on? Explain that type isn't intended to make it easy to label others or to brand them with their weaknesses but to give each of us insight for our own personal growth.

NEXT SESSION

Have your youth read *Find Your Fit* chapter 5—and do the exercises—to prep for your next session.

SESSION FIVE
VALUES

DECIDE BETWEEN GOOD, BETTER, AND BEST THINGS

Talking about values helps many youth turn from focusing on how God has gifted them to how they might use their gifts for God's goals. Talking about passions pursues that discussion even further. Not everyone is ready to turn that corner; some will still be trying to understand and accept what they have learned so far about themselves. Work patiently with your youth as they figure out how to pursue God's best for their lives.

As we noted earlier, in a six-session format you might choose to use part of this session to recap spiritual gifts or other areas that need more coverage or question and answer time.

GET IT GOING

Pick and talk through one of these situations to begin to highlight what your youth value most.

- Burning House: If your house was burning, what would you grab?
- You've Got Money to Give: Split into groups of four. Pretend you have $100,000 to give to some good cause. What three groups will get a portion of your money?

From those discussions, ask the group what a "value" is. Are values always about right and wrong? Or are they also about choosing between good, better, and best?

TALK IT UP

Check out chapter 5 to prepare a talk introducing values. Your key point: Everyone has a set of somewhat flexible values that hugely affect how he or she spends time, energy, and resources.

Offer answers to the following questions:

- What are values? What kind of values are we talking about choosing?
- What was said earlier in the book (pages 19–20) about God's non-negotiables—God's clear commands in the bumper-car rink of life? What does that have to do with values?
- Related illustration of the same point: How are values like two wings of a plane?
- To what extent can a Christian choose his or her values?
- How does a good value "go extreme" and become a bad value?
- How did the Bible's King David have his values in his head and heart yet abandon them in his behavior?
- How do you handle values clashes with parents or others in authority over you?

Some additional points:

- Being aware of their values helps people understand their priorities, clarify their choices, and discern what will give meaning to their lives.
- God wants to *influence* values. Values aren't *given* by God in the same way as spiritual gifts and personality type.
- Awareness of their top eight to ten values helps youth work through conflicts and understand situations that often trouble them the most. Values become most evident in conflict situations.
- People's values can change over their lifetime due to circumstances.

WORK IT OUT

You have a couple options for the rest of your session:

- **Values Card Sort.** If your students haven't been

prereading chapters prior to your sessions, go ahead and do the values card sort exercise (pages 150–151). Give the participants room to spread out their values cards found at the back of *Find Your Fit*. Using the instructions on page 150–151, explain how to set up their prompt cards. Warn your students in advance that it may be hard to limit their top values to eight—but gently make them do it anyway! When they have completed their sort, have them record their values on the Values Summary Page (page 152).

Note: If you are using the *Find Your Fit Discovery Workbook*, you can use REPRODUCIBLE MASTER 36 to accomplish the job of ranking values.

Hint: Although this is an individual exercise, people enjoy sorting their cards while interacting with others. Everyone approaches the sorting task differently and a group atmosphere adds encouragement to what can be a difficult task for some.

Another hint: If some students have worked ahead, it's okay to have them re-sort their cards—it's a helpful way to see which values are consistent from sort to sort, and which need to be rethought because they merely reflected a temporary mood.

- **Values Discussion.** You can also have an extended discussion of how values shape our everyday life. If your students have done the card sort, have them think more deeply about what they learned:
  * Are these the values you want to hold?
  * Are they the same or different from your peers' or family's values?
  * When have you been in a job or classroom situation that clashed with your values?
  * What concrete steps can you take to live out your values?
  * Pick other questions on pages 158–159 as they seem appropriate to your group.

WRAP IT UP

Allow time for questions. Continue to cover the "So Where Do You Go From Here?" section (pages 158–159) as best fits your group.

You may want to encourage your youth to draft a personal mission statement. (Suggestions for a teen-appropriate format are on *Find Your Fit* pages 205–206.) Consider scheduling a help session for those who are interested in pursuing this.

Consider, too, scheduling individual time with students who need to talk through issues raised in *Find Your Fit*. By now your discussions may have triggered a rethinking of future school or career choices; an awareness of the negative effect of bad "sex, drugs, and rock and roll" types of values choices; or a feeling of "So that's why I don't get along with my parents!"

You might want to poll student interest in a special group just to consider future post-high-school-graduation choices.

NEXT SESSION

Have your youth read *Find Your Fit* chapter 6—and do the exercises—to prep for your next session.

SESSION SIX
PASSIONS

COMMIT YOURSELF TO THE CAUSES YOU CARE ABOUT MOST

Passions set youth free to dream. Once they've figured out what they're good at (talents and spiritual gifts), where they function best (personality type), and the needs of the day (values), they can look at the good works God prepared in advance for each of them (Ephesians 2:10). Youth have the advantage of not yet being trapped in many of the day-to-day pressures that prevent adults from dreaming and doing something about helping others or improving society.

Help your students be open-minded to discovering what God has put in their hearts, whether it's big, small, or totally world-shaking.

GET IT GOING

Few youth are apathetic. Even those who seem alienated and uncaring are guided—or misguided—by issues of right and wrong, good and bad, fair and unfair. Tap into some of that passion with one of these choices:

- **Newspaper Scan.** Hand out several newspapers—the news section, that is. What kinds of stories bother you the most? Do you find any stories about children or youth—and if you do, are they good or bad? Do you find any reporting of what youth are doing to change the world?
- **We're Making a Difference.** If you're ready to jump-start your group's thinking about serving, bring in some youth who've already found a place and a cause where they're eager to serve in the church, community, school, etc.
- **If I Had One Wish for the World.** What was the most fulfilling thing you've ever done—spiritual or not? What's the thing you had to work hardest at and did well? If you could do one act of good to make the world a better place, what would it be? What would you give up almost anything to help fix? What little piece of that can you do now?

TALK IT UP

Check out chapter 6 to prepare a talk about passions. Your key point: Even after you discover all sorts of things about yourself, you still have a choice. Are you going to use your gifts selfishly, or for the great purposes God intends?

- God doesn't expect us to act like superheroes. But God does want us to impact our world near and far.
- Serving others may seem like a losing way to approach life. In reality, it's the most satisfying.
- Discuss what passion means. REPRODUCIBLE MASTER 37 defines the word as well as the phrase *en theos*. Use REPRODUCIBLE MASTER 38 to remind students that they are God's masterpieces—and that God gave them incredible gifts to do His work in the world.
- Talk through the things that *don't* have to happen before your youth launch into their passions. Use REPRODUCIBLE MASTER 39 to highlight your points.
- Talk about ways youth you know have shown passion and made a difference in their world.
- Discuss the four ways people discover what they really care about (pages 169–170). REPRODUCIBLE MASTER 40 lists these four approaches to finding passions.

WORK IT OUT

You have some options depending on the needs of your group:

- **Discover Your Passions.** As you start winding down *Find Your Fit* it might be getting harder to get youth to get their homework done before class. You may want to have youth work individually through the exercises on pages 172–178. They can reassemble in small groups to talk about what they discovered.
- **Get Going as a Group.** Talk to your group about ways they can get involved in service. Is there a service opportunity that appeals to your whole group? Or is there a *range* of opportunities you can supply—even in a smaller church—by partnering with existing adult ministries inside and outside church walls? Kevin's book *Catch the Wave!* is a whole book devoted to ways youth can get involved in God's big stuff. It lists loads of examples for school, the community, and the great big world. For many students, it's the perfect follow-up to *Find Your Fit*.
- **Figure Out Rory's Story.** If your youths' brains are bulging and they're wishing God would just tell them what to do, read Rory's Story (*Find Your Fit* chapter 8) and talk through our weird points (pages 201–203).
- **Time Out for Time Management.** If your students have already figured out what they're good at, talk through the principles of *Find Your Fit* chapter 7, "How Not to Spin in Your Socks." This can become an added session depending on your students' needs.
- **Think Deeply.** Ask yourselves what you can do to make your dreams a reality—not just a pretty list of "things I'd like to do someday." Deep questions: If you have a career in mind, how will your passions be a part of that? How will serving God figure into your future? Are there choices you can make right now to help you balance those two things—career and a higher calling?

WRAP IT UP

Make time for celebration as you finish up *Find Your Fit*.

- Throw a party! Wherever two or three Christian youth are gathered, a snack will be served.
- Put on a celebration service with parents.
- Whether during session six or at a party or service, have students summarize what they've recorded on page 207. What were the biggest surprises? What's making the most immediate difference in their lives? What new thing does God have for them to do?
- End with a commitment. Provide students with colorful stationery, stickers, and markers to write a letter to themselves. Have them write about
    * What I learned about myself
    * What steps I'm going to take to learn more about what God wants me to do

    Give them each an envelope to address to themselves. Have them seal their letters. Collect them in an offering basket and mail them to the students 4–6 weeks after your last session.
- You may want to schedule a specific follow-up session in a few weeks for students to ask questions and talk about what they're doing to act on what they learned in *Find Your Fit*.

FIND YOUR FIT

PSALM 139:14

"THANK YOU FOR MAKING ME SO WONDERFULLY COMPLEX!

YOUR WORKMANSHIP IS MARVELOUS."

NEW LIVING TRANSLATION

FIND YOUR FIT HELPS YOU DISCOVER

YOUR TALENTS
The assortment of things you do well

YOUR SPIRITUAL GIFTS
Your abilities that let you be part of God's big purposes

YOUR PERSONALITY TYPE
Your built-in preferences for how you get energized, take in information, make decisions, and steer your life

YOUR VALUES
Your rankings of what is most important to you

YOUR PASSIONS
The causes, issues, and interests you care about deeply

REPRODUCIBLE MASTER 2

Find Your Fit Leader's Guide © 2000. Permission granted to reproduce this page for workshop use. Any other use, including resale, is prohibited.

FIND YOUR FIT

REALISTIC TYPE

THINGS YOU DO OR DREAM ABOUT sports, hunting, fishing, camping, rock climbing, rafting; training animals; working on or operating cars, boats, planes, etc.

PEOPLE SEE YOU AS reliable, outdoorsy, athletic, mechanical, hands-on

YOU MIGHT SPEND MONEY ON cars, camping equipment, fising and hunting licenses

SOME TYPICAL CAREER INTERESTS engineer, forester, race-car driver, pilot, military officer, athletic trainer, animal trainer

YOUR HEROES Tim "The Toolman" Allen, Amelia Earhart (explorer), Indiana Jones, Rocky

THINGS YOU GET IN TROUBLE AT SCHOOL FOR blowing off any work you don't see as useful in "real life"

INVESTIGATIVE TYPE

THINGS YOU DO OR DREAM ABOUT scientific research, computer programming, going on an archaeological dig, mastering complex hobbies like skiing or chess

PEOPLE SEE YOU AS curious, scholarly, intellectual, independent, original

YOU MIGHT SPEND MONEY ON books; complex hobbies like astronomy, sailing, or rock climbing; computers or stereos—and upgrades, upgrades, upgrades!

SOME TYPICAL CAREER INTERESTS chemist, physician, psychologist, science teacher, college professor, computer programmer

YOUR HEROES Nancy Drew, Albert Einstein, Madam Curie, Bill Nye the Science Guy

THINGS YOU GET IN TROUBLE AT SCHOOL FOR ignoring any school subject you aren't hotly interested in so you can spend loads of time on things you like—and dissecting animals you aren't supposed to

REPRODUCIBLE MASTER 3

Find Your Fit Leader's Guide © 2000. Permission granted to reproduce this page for workshop use. Any other use, including resale, is prohibited.

ARTISTIC TYPE

THINGS YOU DO OR DREAM ABOUT acting or performing musically; painting, sculpting, photography; reporting for the school newspaper; writing; going to concerts

PEOPLE SEE YOU AS non-conformist, creative, musical or artistic, expressive, sensitive

YOU MIGHT SPEND MONEY ON tickets to museums or theatres, art supplies, original clothing

SOME TYPICAL CAREER INTERESTS photographer, artist, musician—but also attorney, reporter, public relations director, minister

YOUR HEROES Ansel Adams, Laura Ashley, George Lucas, Bill Shakespeare, Bill Cosby

THINGS YOU GET IN TROUBLE AT SCHOOL FOR daydreaming, insisting on self-expression and uniqueness, producing beautiful projects that don't follow directions

SOCIAL TYPE

THINGS YOU DO OR DREAM ABOUT organizing parties, traveling with friends, volunteer work, religious activities, being a foreign exchange student, working with kids

PEOPLE SEE YOU AS helpful, cooperative, friendly, kind, a good listener

YOU MIGHT SPEND MONEY ON extracurricular activities, going out with friends, hobbies that let you be with others, and "self-discovery" classes

SOME TYPICAL CAREER INTERESTS elementary school teacher, social worker, park and recreation coordinator, physical therapist, nurse, counselor

YOUR HEROES Mother Teresa, Princess Diana, Kofi Annan (head of the United Nations)

THINGS YOU GET IN TROUBLE AT SCHOOL FOR jabbering, passing notes, and planning parties when the teacher is talking

REPRODUCIBLE MASTER 4

FIND YOUR FIT

ENTERPRISING TYPE

THINGS YOU DO OR DREAM ABOUT being president—preferably of the country, being part of the "in" crowd, debating and persuading, running a business, enjoying "the good life"

PEOPLE SEE YOU AS persuasive, self-confident, extroverted, risk-taker, ambitious

YOU MIGHT SPEND MONEY ON the latest and greatest clothes, tickets to the biggest concerts, or any of the finer things in life

SOME TYPICAL CAREER INTERESTS sales, management, marketing, lobbyist, financial planner, TV announcer, politician

YOUR HEROES Bill Gates, Billy Graham, Margaret Thatcher

THINGS YOU GET IN TROUBLE AT SCHOOL FOR scheming your way through school—sweet-talking others into doing all the work on group projects, selling candy during study hall, scamming the principal out of his sweet parking spot

CONVENTIONAL TYPE

THINGS YOU DO OR DREAM ABOUT collecting anything and everything, sight-seeing, visiting popular historic or amusement sites, owning a cabin, living an orderly life

PEOPLE SEE YOU AS practical, methodical, efficient, content, accurate

YOU MIGHT SPEND MONEY ON you don't—you save for homes, college, big-ticket items

SOME TYPICAL CAREER INTERESTS accountant, banker, office manager, production manager, business education or mathematics teacher

YOUR HEROES Cal Ripken—baseball's most dependable player, Miss Manners—who knows which fork to use at a fancy dinner, Mister Rogers—always wore the same sweater

THINGS YOU GET IN TROUBLE AT SCHOOL FOR You don't get in trouble unless it's for telling on kids getting into trouble. You're usually the one who asks, "Is this going to be on the test?" (a question the rest of us love you for)

REPRODUCIBLE MASTER 5

Find Your Fit Leader's Guide © 2000. Permission granted to reproduce this page for workshop use. Any other use, including resale, is prohibited.

SPIRITUAL GIFTS BINGO

FIND YOUR FIT

Circle the statements that apply to you—then collect on each square as many initials as you can from others in your group.

I can sit on the phone for hours listening to a friend's problems	I've sung in a nursing home	When I grow up I want to be president—of anything!	I've told friends Jesus could help them and some didn't gag	I think mean people are, well, really mean	I read the back of cereal boxes
I like to baby-sit and know how to wipe up all forms of baby slime	I know how to take down a folding table	I led the charge to beat up the neighborhood bully	People ask me what brand of computer, car, or clothes to buy	More than once I've told my friends or co-workers, "This isn't right"	My teachers are boring and/or stupid and I could do a better job
I've served food at a soup kitchen	I'd rather pass out programs than sing on stage	I've helped plan events, meetings, and/or social activities	If forced to choose, I'd rather discuss philosophy than eat pizza	I think the Bible applies to my everyday life	I've taught (or helped teach) Sunday school—and lived
I don't flip the channel when a "starving children" infomercial comes on	I blush when I'm the center of attention	I often decide where my group of friends should go or what we should do	I've gone on a missions project	My gut tells me right from wrong	People listen to what I have to say, mostly
People like to come to parties at my house	I hold the door for people	I'm a control freak—or just like being in charge	I'm not embarrassed for people to know I go to church	My parents have never had to ask me, "If all your friends were jumping off a cliff, would you?"	I have a library card and I'm not afraid to use it

REPRODUCIBLE MASTER 6

Find Your Fit Leader's Guide © 2000. Permission granted to reproduce this page for workshop use. Any other use, including resale, is prohibited.

THE GIFT OF EVANGELISM

The ability to spread the Good News of Jesus Christ in a way that appeals to those who don't know Him—causing people to know and follow Jesus.

- I can comfortably talk about my Christian faith with others in a way that makes them comfortable.
- I wish others could understand why my faith is so important to me.
- I enjoy many friendships with people who aren't Christians.
- I enjoy studying questions that challenge Christianity.
- I look for ways to help people understand how their needs can be met through Christianity.

THE GIFT OF HELPS

The ability to work alongside others, seeing spiritual value in the practical tasks that further God's purposes.

- I don't need to be a leader—I'd rather take on practical tasks.
- I notice little jobs that need to be done and do them.
- When I help with routine tasks, I feel a spiritual link to the ministries or people I serve.
- Quietly serving others is fulfilling to me.
- I like working behind the scenes and dislike being praised in public for my efforts.

THE GIFT OF LEADERSHIP

The ability to motivate, coordinate, and direct others in doing God's work.

- Disorganization frustrates me; I want to take over.
- If I'm in charge, my friends sense we're headed in the right direction.
- I'm in control of my own time/priorities *or* my own belongings *or* finances.
- I like to organize facts, people, or events.
- I can lay out the actions needed to deal with anticipated problems.

THE GIFTS OF DISCERNMENT AND PROPHECY

The ability to recognize what comes from God and what doesn't—or to proclaim God's truths in ways that fit current situations, with insight into how God wants things to change.

- I often get a gut feel whether a situation is good or bad.
- I can judge where people are coming from—whether they're real or fake.
- I sense whether a book/movie/presentation will bring people closer to God—or push them away.
- Sometimes I see or think of images that convey God's truth.
- I listen carefully for what God wants me to say to others.

FIND YOUR FIT

THE GIFTS OF ENCOURAGEMENT AND MERCY

The ability to see the suffering of others and offer comfort by showing empathy, listening effectively, or acting kindly—helping them heal emotionally, relationally, or physically.

- I get upset when others are hurt or rejected. I want to reach out to them.
- I like to show others how much God loves them.
- Others say I'm a good listener.
- I often see the best in others—things they're slow to recognize in themselves.
- I see how I can help others and can gain their confidence easily.

REPRODUCIBLE MASTER 11

FIND YOUR FIT

THE GIFT OF FAITH

The ability to recognize what God wants accomplished—a strong belief that God will see it done no matter how big the barriers.

- I know God is faithful even when life seems impossible.
- I firmly believe God is active in our lives.
- My friends tell me I'm an "incurable optimist."
- If I sense that God is behind a project or idea, I can support it even when others are doubtful.
- My personal experiences help me believe in the power of faith.

REPRODUCIBLE MASTER 12

FIND YOUR FIT

THE GIFT OF GIVING

The ability to give of material possessions freely and happily to assist people and further God's causes.

- I handle money well.
- No one has to push me to give to others.
- It's easy for me to ask others to give to causes I believe in.
- I've had creative ideas that helped my family give more money to others.
- Giving to a cause or ministry helps me feel a part of it.

FIND YOUR FIT

THE GIFT OF HOSPITALITY

The ability to demonstrate God's love by providing others with a warm welcome, food, shelter, or fellowship.

- I can make all kinds of people feel welcome.
- I make an effort to connect with new kids at church or school.
- I seem to know what activities or food will appeal to others.
- If I help with arrangements for a party or event, I think less about what I want than what will make others feel welcome.
- I see relationships as opportunities to pass on God's love.

THE GIFT OF
TEACHING

The ability to understand and communicate God's truths to others effectively—so that truth changes lives.

- I enjoy studying the Bible and other resources that help me learn about God.
- I like to learn about new ideas, gathering information so I can pass it on to others.
- I want to relate God's truth to life in a way that helps people grow and develop—not to skewer them with truth but to help them.
- When I study or hear other teachers, I automatically think about how I might teach the information to others.
- When I talk about what I've learned, others often want to learn more about God.

FIND YOUR FIT

THE GIFTS OF TONGUES, HEALING, AND MIRACLES

The ability to function in ways that are unexpected and even miraculous—not for the sake of bringing attention to yourself but to demonstrate God's power.

- I sometimes pray in a language I have never heard before.
- I pray for things obviously beyond the natural capacity of people.
- I expectantly ask God to heal people who are sick.
- I have seen God work through me in miraculous ways I can't explain.
- I focus attention on God, not myself.

REPRODUCIBLE MASTER 16

Find Your Fit Leader's Guide © 2000. Permission granted to reproduce this page for workshop use. Any other use, including resale, is prohibited.

FIND YOUR FIT

DISCOVERING YOUR SPIRITUAL GIFTS

Read the following statements, scoring each one as follows:

1 = Definitely not one of my gifts.
2 = Not sure. Haven't tried this, but it sounds interesting.
3 = One of my gifts—I know it.

THE GIFT OF EVANGELISM

The ability to spread the Good News of Jesus Christ in a way that appeals to those who don't know Him—causing people to know and follow Jesus.

- ☐ I can comfortably talk about my Christian faith with others in a way that makes them comfortable as well.
- ☐ I wish others could understand why my faith is so important to me.
- ☐ I enjoy many friendships with people who aren't Christians.
- ☐ I enjoy studying questions that challenge Christianity.
- ☐ I look for ways to help people understand how their needs can be met through Christianity.

My score (1, 2, or 3): _____

THE GIFT OF LEADERSHIP

The ability to motivate, coordinate, and direct others in doing God's work.

- ☐ Disorganization frustrates me; I want to take over.
- ☐ If I'm in charge, my friends sense we're headed in the right direction.
- ☐ I'm in control of my own time/priorities *or* my own belongings *or* finances.
- ☐ I like to organize facts, people, or events.
- ☐ I can lay out the actions needed to deal with anticipated problems.

My score (1, 2, or 3): _____

THE GIFT OF HELPS

The ability to work alongside others, seeing spiritual value in the practical tasks that further God's purposes.

- ☐ I don't need to be a leader—I'd rather take on practical tasks.
- ☐ I notice little jobs that need to be done and do them.
- ☐ When I help with routine tasks, I feel a spiritual link to the ministries or people I serve.
- ☐ Quietly serving others is fulfilling to me.
- ☐ I like working behind the scenes and dislike being praised in public for my efforts.

My score (1, 2, or 3): _____

THE GIFTS OF DISCERNMENT AND PROPHECY

The ability to recognize what comes from God and what doesn't—or to proclaim God's truths in ways that fit current situations, with insight into how God wants things to change.

- ☐ I often get a gut feeling whether a situation is good or bad.
- ☐ I can judge where people are coming from— whether they're real or fake.
- ☐ I sense whether a book/movie/presentation will bring people closer to God—or push them away.
- ☐ Sometimes I see or think of images that convey God's truth.
- ☐ I listen carefully for what God wants me to say to others.

My score (1, 2, or 3): _____

REPRODUCIBLE MASTER 17

Find Your Fit Leader's Guide © 2000. Permission granted to reproduce this page for workshop use. Any other use, including resale, is prohibited.

FIND YOUR FIT

THE GIFTS OF ENCOURAGEMENT AND MERCY

The ability to see the suffering of others and offer comfort by showing empathy, listening effectively, or acting kindly—helping them heal emotionally, relationally, or physically.

- ☐ I get upset when others are hurt or rejected. I want to reach out to them.
- ☐ I like to show others how much God loves them.
- ☐ Others say I'm a good listener.
- ☐ I often see the best in others—things they're slow to recognize in themselves.
- ☐ I see how I can help others and can gain their confidence easily.

My score (1, 2, or 3): _____

THE GIFT OF HOSPITALITY

The ability to demonstrate God's love by providing others with a warm welcome, food, shelter, or fellowship.

- ☐ I can make all kinds of people feel welcome.
- ☐ I make an effort to connect with new kids at church or school.
- ☐ I seem to know what activities or food will appeal to others.
- ☐ If I help with arrangements for a party or event, I think less about what I want than what will make others feel welcome.
- ☐ I see relationships as opportunities to pass on God's love.

My score (1, 2, or 3): _____

THE GIFT OF FAITH

The ability to recognize what God wants accomplished—a strong belief that God will see it done no matter how big the barriers.

- ☐ I know God is faithful even when life seems impossible.
- ☐ I firmly believe God is active in our lives.
- ☐ My friends tell me I'm an "incurable optimist."
- ☐ If I sense that God is behind a project or idea, I can support it even when others are doubtful.
- ☐ My personal experiences help me believe in the power of faith.

My score (1, 2, or 3): _____

THE GIFT OF TEACHING

The ability to understand and communicate God's truths to others effectively—so that truth changes lives.

- ☐ I enjoy studying the Bible and other resources that help me learn about God.
- ☐ I like to learn about new ideas, gathering information so I can pass it on to others.
- ☐ I want to relate God's truth to life in a way that helps people grow and develop—not to skewer them with truth but to help them.
- ☐ When I study or hear other teachers, I automatically think about how I might teach the information to others.
- ☐ When I talk about what I've learned, others often want to learn more about God.

My score (1, 2, or 3): _____

THE GIFT OF GIVING

The ability to give of material possessions freely and happily to assist people and further God's causes.

- ☐ I handle money well.
- ☐ No one has to push me to give to others.
- ☐ It's easy for me to ask others to give to causes I believe in.
- ☐ I've had creative ideas that helped my family give more money to others.
- ☐ Giving to a cause or ministry helps me feel a part of it.

My score (1, 2, or 3): _____

THE GIFT OF TONGUES, HEALING, AND MIRACLES

The ability to function in ways that are unexpected and even miraculous—not for the sake of bringing attention to yourself but to demonstrate God's power.

- ☐ I sometimes pray in a language I have never heard before.
- ☐ I pray for things obviously beyond the natural capacity of people.
- ☐ I expectantly ask God to heal people who are sick.
- ☐ I have seen God work through me in miraculous ways I can't explain.
- ☐ I focus attention on God, not myself.

My score (1, 2, or 3): _____

REPRODUCIBLE MASTER 18

Find Your Fit Leader's Guide © 2000. Permission granted to reproduce this page for workshop use. Any other use, including resale, is prohibited.

MY FRIEND MEGAN

Megan is a ninth-grade friend whose dad just died after a long battle with cancer. Besides Megan, her family includes a fourth grader, a second grader, and a preschooler. Megan's mom works three afternoons a week and has no close family in the area.

Megan is angry that she has to care for the younger kids so much—not to mention the fact that she feels hurt over her dad's death. She's had to drop out of after-school activities because she can't find a ride home, and her grades are slipping.

Two questions to answer individually—and then as a group:

1. List a few of the needs Megan's family would have. Choose the one you would be most interested in responding to. Describe what you would do to help.
2. Share your responses as a group. How do the various responses reflect your differing spiritual gifts? Your life gifts?

WHAT IS "PSYCHOLOGICAL TYPE"?

- Type explains *observable differences* in people.

- Type describes *natural preferences* for how people get energized, take in information, make decisions, and steer their lives.

- Type describes *settings* where people might most readily put their talents and spiritual gifts to use.

- No type preference is better than another—just different.

- Type is not an excuse.

- Type experts believe people are *born* a certain type—but that people can still...
  - act on their strengths
  - work on their weaknesses
  - learn to "step out of their box."

FIND YOUR FIT

EXTRAVERSION AND INTROVERSION

HOW YOU ARE ENERGIZED—
BY THE OUTSIDE WORLD OR THE INSIDE WORLD

1. You find out a group is going to the beach. Which sounds more like you?

   Extraverts might
   - ☐ Sit with all sorts of different people throughout the day
   - ☐ Jump in with a joke or new idea if there's a lull in conversation
   - ☐ Join the group in whatever activity you can

   Introverts might
   - ☐ Stick with one or two close friends for most of the day
   - ☐ Get lost in thought when there's a lull in conversation
   - ☐ Join the group only if you've tried the activity before or if one or two of your close friends join you

2. You're supposed to work with a group on a project. Which describes your approach to the task?

   Extraverts might
   - ☐ Have fun working as a group
   - ☐ Turn the group sessions into a chance to socialize
   - ☐ Share ideas readily

   Introverts might
   - ☐ Divvy up the assignment so you can do your part alone
   - ☐ Keep the group sessions shorter unless working with a close friend
   - ☐ Share ideas when asked

TIE-BREAKER QUESTION: How do you do your homework?

   At the kitchen table or where the action is (Extraverts)
   In your room away from distractions (Introverts)

DEEP THOUGHTS ABOUT EXTRAVERSION AND INTROVERSION:

- These preferences aren't about sociability and shyness. Rather, it's whether you get charged up being around other people or are ready to retreat after a lot of contact with others.
- In the U.S., 30–40 percent of the population is introverted, yet teens may feel pressured to say they are extraverted since they may equate it with popularity.
- This isn't either/or, but which is most natural.

REPRODUCIBLE MASTER 21

Find Your Fit Leader's Guide © 2000. Permission granted to reproduce this page for workshop use. Any other use, including resale, is prohibited.

FIND YOUR FIT

SENSING AND INTUITION

HOW YOU TAKE IN INFORMATION AND SEE THE WORLD— DETAILS OR THE BIG PICTURE

1. Your teacher assigns a report on Greek mythology. How would you tackle it?

   Sensors might
   - ☐ Ask for a list of suggested topics
   - ☐ Want to know the requirements for an A, B, or C grade—and do what you have to for the grade you want
   - ☐ Regurgitate the facts you know the teacher wants

   Intuitives might
   - ☐ Brainstorm your own topic
   - ☐ Write what you want
   - ☐ Go searching where no student has ever gone before.

2. You're with a group of friends at lunch, discussing what you did over the weekend. How would you describe your days?

   Sensors might
   - ☐ Start by telling what you did Friday night, then continue in order to Saturday morning, afternoon, evening, etc.
   - ☐ Tell facts about where you went and what you did
   - ☐ Fill your weekends with activities you know you enjoy

   Intuitives might
   - ☐ Start with whatever comes to mind first, then jump around from day to day
   - ☐ Jump from the facts to ideas you had or what you might like to do next
   - ☐ Try to find new things to do or experience

TIE-BREAKER QUESTION: How do you do with details?

> You know all the street names to give directions to your house or school (Sensors)
>
> You give directions using landmarks and guesstimates (Intuitives)

DEEP THOUGHTS ABOUT SENSING AND INTUITION:

- ■ This is about the kind of information that you're attracted to: Do you see the forest or the trees?
- ■ You might think about what messes you up in schoolwork the most, not being careful or checking your work in arithmetic or spelling (where Intuitives struggle) OR having more trouble understanding the theories or big concepts (where Sensors struggle).
- ■ As high as 75 percent of the U.S. population reports a preference for Sensing.

REPRODUCIBLE MASTER 22

Find Your Fit Leader's Guide © 2000. Permission granted to reproduce this page for workshop use. Any other use, including resale, is prohibited.

FIND YOUR FIT

THINKING AND FEELING

HOW YOU MAKE DECISIONS— WITH YOUR HEAD OR WITH YOUR HEART

1. Summer is coming and Mom or Dad says you have to find something to do—either a part-time job or a volunteer position to keep you busy.

   Thinkers might
   - ☐ Set goals or objectives for your summer activities
   - ☐ Decide on objective criteria—hours, pay, store discounts
   - ☐ Choose something that will add to your résumé

   Feelers might
   - ☐ Decide what might be meaningful to you for the summer
   - ☐ Check out what your friends are doing and see if you can join them
   - ☐ Choose something that allows you to help people

2. It's the start of a new school year, time to meet all the new teachers. How do you separate the good teachers from the bad?

   Thinkers might
   - ☐ Look first for what's *wrong* with the teacher (dress, organization, quality of assignments)
   - ☐ Be concerned with how competent the teacher is
   - ☐ Want information presented in a logical, concise manner

   Feelers might
   - ☐ Look first for what's *right* with the teacher
   - ☐ Be concerned with whether the teacher likes you
   - ☐ Want information presented in a personal way

TIE-BREAKER QUESTION: When your friend has a problem, do you . . .

   Give advice (Thinkers)
   Give comfort (Feelers)

DEEP THOUGHTS ABOUT THINKING AND FEELING:

- ■ Thinkers have feelings, Feeling types think. This is about how we prefer to make decisions. T's want to be logical, objective, while F's put themselves in the shoes of the people involved to see what would be best.
- ■ There are about as many T's as F's in the U.S. However, there are more male T's (60 percent) and more female F's (75 percent).
- ■ The best decisions are balanced decisions—we need to consider both rules and the people involved.

REPRODUCIBLE MASTER 23

FIND YOUR FIT

JUDGING AND PERCEIVING

HOW YOU RUN YOUR LIFE—
YOU PLAN YOUR LIFE OR YOU GO WITH THE FLOW

1. It's Friday, the weekend's coming, and everyone is grabbing stuff at work or at school and heading out the door. How do you approach the two days ahead?

   Judgers might
   - ☐ Schedule exactly when you'll do your homework/tasks
   - ☐ Study the TV or movie schedule and plan your day so you can watch a certain show
   - ☐ Make set plans for Saturday with a friend before leaving work or school—plans guarantee a good time

   Perceivers might
   - ☐ Do your homework when you feel like it
   - ☐ Turn on the TV and flip channels when you feel like it
   - ☐ Start calling friends sometime Saturday and go wherever with whoever's available—plans might keep you from a better option

2. You're about to buy a new "toy"—a CD player, a car, or video camera. How do you go about making a decision?

   Judgers might
   - ☐ Limit how long you'll spend shopping
   - ☐ Reach your decision quickly—even before you have all the facts
   - ☐ Not second-guess your choice once you've bought it

   Perceivers might
   - ☐ Shop as long as needed to check out all the options
   - ☐ Get as much input from friends and experts as possible—even postpone your decision
   - ☐ Revisit your decision if you find out new information

TIE-BREAKER QUESTION When you order at a restaurant, do you...

> Make a quick decision (Judgers)
> Look at what everyone else is eating, ask your server for recommendations, go to the kitchen and talk to the cook—and keep looking at the menu after you have ordered (Perceivers)

DEEP THOUGHTS ABOUT JUDGING AND PERCEIVING:

- Judging types are NOT judgmental. Perceiving types are NOT more perceptive.
- Think about when you do your best work—when you have plenty of time (J) or when you're under deadline pressure (P).
- In the U.S. population, there are more Judging types (60 percent) than Perceiving types, but school and work environments emphasize the goal-setting, schedule-oriented Judging style.

REPRODUCIBLE MASTER 24

Find Your Fit Leader's Guide © 2000. Permission granted to reproduce this page for workshop use. Any other use, including resale, is prohibited.

FORCED CHOICE OPTION 2: LIVING TYPE TABLE

STEP 1: **Stand at the front of the room.** Summarize the descriptions of Extraverts and Introverts on pages 91–93 (both the longer descriptions and the "Summing Up" parts are helpful, with the examples good for clarification). Have those with a preference for Introversion move to the front of the room toward where you are standing and those with a preference for Extraversion move to the back. Place a masking tape line between the E's and I's. Say a few words about E and I at school: being graded on class participation, group projects, and expectations about popularity all often favor extraversion.

STEP 2: **Divide the room again, this time with "left" and "right" sides.** Summarize the descriptions of Sensing and Intuition on pages 94–97. Ask everyone to stay where they are in regard to the top and bottom of the room, but have those with a preference for Intuition move to the right side of the room. Again place a masking tape line to separate the two groups. This now creates four quadrants. (Check out the type table on Reproducible Master page 27 to make sure you give the right directions.) Mention the following:

- Those in the IS (top left) quadrant enjoy settings that honor past experience: What's worked for us before? What's practical? Show me step by step what to do.
- Those in the EN (bottom right) quadrant enjoy settings that honor change and innovation: We've already done it that way. Let's do something different this time. Change is better—trust me.
- Those in the IN (top right) quadrant enjoy settings where they can develop and promote the ideas that call for change: Let's think about this, come up with new ideas. What could be different?
- Those in the ES (bottom left) quadrant enjoy settings that are action-oriented, seeking to change or improve on something: Let's just do it. Stop the talk and start acting.

Those four main divisions highlight some major differences in how people approach life. Another step:

REPRODUCIBLE MASTER 25

FIND YOUR FIT

STEP 3: With the masking tape, divide the room into four "columns," with two on the right and two on the left side of the room. Then have those with a preference for Thinking move to the outer left or right columns; those with a preference for Feeling are to move to the inner columns. Again, refer to Reproducible Master 27 to see how the T-F division is made.

- Those in the ST column concentrate on the present and on the specific facts: What do the facts tell me about how to fix the problem in the most practical way? Give me practical things to do with data, things, procedures—where I can see the results and know when things turn out right.
- Those in the SF column also concentrate on the present and specific facts: How can I use this information to help the people around me feel better today? Let me meet the needs of the person right in front of me in the kindest, most efficient way.
- Those in the NF column concentrate on the future and the big picture: How can I use this information to help people realize their potential? How can I change things to make things better for people and the organizations that serve them?
- Those in the NT column also concentrate on the future and the big picture: How does this help me understand the system, its structure, or grasp a universal truth? How can I change the system to solve the big problem?

STEP 4: And one last step. Divide each of the top and bottom portions of the room into two rows each with the masking tape. Have those with a preference for Judging move to the very bottom and the very top rows, where they can help "keep order." Have those with a preference for Perceiving stay in the middle two rows. This last division puts people in the 16 types described in MBTI© theory.

- You can now use the *Find Your Fit* type descriptions (pages 110–141) to come up with at least one nice thing to say about each type. For example, "ISTJ's do what they said they'd do and keep the rest of us organized!"

REPRODUCIBLE MASTER 26

FIND YOUR FIT

TYPE TABLE

ISTJ	ISFJ	INFJ	INTJ
ISTP	ISFP	INFP	INTP
ESTP	ESFP	ENFP	ENTP
ESTJ	ESFJ	ENFJ	ENTJ

REPRODUCIBLE MASTER 27

Find Your Fit Leader's Guide © 2000. Permission granted to reproduce this page for workshop use. Any other use, including resale, is prohibited.

FIND YOUR FIT

EXTRAVERSION

*Your energy comes from
being with others
or from
many activities*

INTROVERSION

*Your energy comes from
time away from others
or a few
indepth activities*

REPRODUCIBLE MASTER 28

Find Your Fit Leader's Guide © 2000. Permission granted to reproduce this page for workshop use. Any other use, including resale, is prohibited.

FIND YOUR FIT

WHERE DO YOU GET YOUR ENERGY?

EXTRAVERSION

- Doing; lots going on
- Like interruptions
- Outgoing
- Invite others in
- Say what you're thinking
- Outer energy
- Act
- Live it first
- Focus outside
- Take over

INTROVERSION

- Reflecting; one thing going on
- Don't like interruptions
- Protective
- Wait to be invited
- Keep thoughts to yourself
- Inner energy
- Reflect
- Understand it first
- Focus inside
- Step aside

REPRODUCIBLE MASTER 29

Find Your Fit Leader's Guide © 2000. Permission granted to reproduce this page for workshop use. Any other use, including resale, is prohibited.

FIND YOUR FIT

SENSING

*You perceive
what is
—the information
the five senses gather*

INTUITION

*You perceive what
could be
—through hunches, connections,
analogies*

REPRODUCIBLE MASTER 30

Find Your Fit Leader's Guide © 2000. Permission granted to reproduce this page for workshop use. Any other use, including resale, is prohibited.

FIND YOUR FIT

HOW DO YOU TAKE IN INFORMATION?

SENSING

- Practical, common sense
- Accuracy
- Rely on past experience
- Methodical approach
- By (or buy!) the book
- Current reality
- Stick with it until you're done
- Real world
- Applied
- See the trees

INTUITION

- Innovative, insightful
- Creativity
- Rely on fresh inspiration
- New, unusual approach
- Create the book
- Future possibilities
- Stick with it until you find a better way
- Ideal world
- Theoretical
- See the forest

REPRODUCIBLE MASTER 31

FIND YOUR FIT

THINKING

You make decisions based on logic and impartial standards

FEELING

You make decisions by stepping into the shoes of those involved

REPRODUCIBLE MASTER 32

Find Your Fit Leader's Guide © 2000. Permission granted to reproduce this page for workshop use. Any other use, including resale, is prohibited.

FIND YOUR FIT

HOW DO YOU MAKE DECISIONS?

THINKING

- Logical, analytical
- Ideas for data and things
- Fair but firm—no exceptions
- Business first
- Want recognition for *exceeding requirements*
- Quick to give advice
- Decide with the head
- Find the flaw
- Reasons—objective truth

FEELING

- Harmonious, personal
- Ideas for people
- Empathetic—making exceptions
- Friendship first
- Want praise for personal *effort*
- Quick to give comfort
- Decide with the heart
- Find the positive
- Values—personal choice

FIND YOUR FIT

JUDGING

You approach life by planning your work and working your plan

PERCEIVING

You approach life by taking advantage of the moment

REPRODUCIBLE MASTER 34

FIND YOUR FIT

HOW DO YOU PLAN YOUR LIFE?

JUDGING

- Organized, efficient
- Planned events
- Stress reduced by planning ahead
- Settled and decided
- Work before play
- Regular, steady effort
- Systematic
- Scheduled
- Definite selection
- Enjoy finishing

PERCEIVING

- Flexible, multiple tasks
- Impromptu events
- Stress reduced by having options
- Open to late-breaking info
- Work and play at the same time
- Last minute bursts
- Spontaneous
- Spur of the moment
- Several possible choices
- Enjoy starting

REPRODUCIBLE MASTER 35

Find Your Fit Leader's Guide © 2000. Permission granted to reproduce this page for workshop use. Any other use, including resale, is prohibited.

VALUES SORT

INSTRUCTIONS:

Rate each of the values listed below as
1 = This is very important to me.
2 = This is important to me.
3 = This is not very important to me.

BIG NOTE:

You can have no more than 8 values rated as "very important"!

___ Accuracy	___ Cooperation	___ Learning	___ Recognition
___ Achievement	___ Creativity	___ Leisure	___ Relationship With God
___ Advancement	___ Efficiency	___ Location	___ Responsibility
___ Adventure	___ Fairness	___ Love	___ Security
___ Aesthetics	___ Family	___ Loyalty	___ Self-Respect
___ Artistic Expression	___ Financial Security	___ Nature	___ Service
___ Authenticity	___ Flexibility	___ Organization	___ Stability
___ Balance	___ Friendship	___ Peace	___ Tolerance
___ Challenge	___ Generosity	___ Perseverance	___ Tradition
___ Competency	___ Happiness	___ Personal Development	___ Variety
___ Competition	___ Humor	___ Physical Fitness & Health	___ _____
___ Conformity	___ Independence	___ Power	___ _____
___ Contribution	___ Influence	___ Prestige	___ _____
___ Control	___ Integrity	___ Purity	___ _____

In the space below, list your top eight values—and then rank them from 1 to 8, from most valued to least valued.

What are your thoughts about the values you selected? Are you surprised by any?

Which of your top values are influencing decisions you are making right now—about friends, school, your future? How?

Which of your values are causing you conflict or tension?

WHAT'S A PASSION?

- Passion is caring about something bigger than yourself—something vital to you and significant in the grand scheme of things.

- Passion is "a powerful emotion. Fervor ardor, enthusiasm, zeal."

- Enthusiasm is from the Greek phrase *en theos*, or "with God."

- A worthwhile passion is anything you pursue "with God." And anything you pursue with God is truly worthwhile.

EPHESIANS 2:10

"FOR WE ARE GOD'S MASTERPIECE. HE HAS CREATED US ANEW IN CHRIST JESUS, SO THAT WE CAN DO THE GOOD THINGS HE PLANNED FOR US LONG AGO."

NEW LIVING TRANSLATION

YOUR PASSION RATING

- You don't have to be an adult to be passionate about God's causes.

- You don't have to be a minister or missionary to make an impact for God.

- You don't have to change the whole world.

- You don't necessarily have to serve strangers.

- You don't have to act on your passions only through church.

- You don't have to be a religious expert to get started.

- You don't have to save passions for your spare time.

FOUR WAYS TO FIND YOUR PASSION

You probably fit into one of four approaches:

- "Dreamers" have lots of ideas but need to pick the best.

- "Do One Thing Well" people have a talent or spiritual gift they use again and again.

- "Watcha Up To?" people enjoy joining up with a vision other people are pursuing.

- "Drop It in My Lap" people see opportunities to serve all around them.

Unit Conversions (Equivalents)

Length

1 in. = 2.54 cm (defined)
1 cm = 0.3937 in.
1 ft = 30.48 cm
1 m = 39.37 in. = 3.281 ft
1 mi = 5280 ft = 1.609 km
1 km = 0.6214 mi
1 nautical mile (U.S.) = 1.151 mi = 6076 ft = 1.852 km
1 fermi = 1 femtometer (fm) = 10^{-15} m
1 angstrom (Å) = 10^{-10} m = 0.1 nm
1 light-year (ly) = 9.461×10^{15} m
1 parsec = 3.26 ly = 3.09×10^{16} m

Volume

1 liter (L) = 1000 mL = 1000 cm^3 = 1.0×10^{-3} m^3 = 1.057 qt (U.S.) = 61.02 in.^{3}
1 gal (U.S.) = 4 qt (U.S.) = 231 in.^{3} = 3.785 L = 0.8327 gal (British)
1 quart (U.S.) = 2 pints (U.S.) = 946 mL
1 pint (British) = 1.20 pints (U.S.) = 568 mL
1 m^3 = 35.31 ft^3

Speed

1 mi/h = 1.4667 ft/s = 1.6093 km/h = 0.4470 m/s
1 km/h = 0.2778 m/s = 0.6214 mi/h
1 ft/s = 0.3048 m/s = 0.6818 mi/h = 1.0973 km/h
1 m/s = 3.281 ft/s = 3.600 km/h = 2.237 mi/h
1 knot = 1.151 mi/h = 0.5144 m/s

Angle

1 radian (rad) = 57.30° = 57°18'
1° = 0.01745 rad
1 rev/min (rpm) = 0.1047 rad/s

Time

1 day = 8.640×10^4 s
1 year = 365.242 days = 3.156×10^7 s

Mass

1 atomic mass unit (u) = 1.6605×10^{-27} kg
1 kg = 0.06852 slug
[1 kg has a weight of 2.20 lb where g = 9.80 m/s^2.]

Force

1 lb = 4.44822 N
1 N = 10^5 dyne = 0.2248 lb

Energy and Work

1 J = 10^7 ergs = 0.7376 ft·lb
1 ft·lb = 1.356 J = 1.29×10^{-3} Btu = 3.24×10^{-4} kcal
1 kcal = 4.19×10^3 J = 3.97 Btu
1 eV = 1.6022×10^{-19} J
1 kWh = 3.600×10^6 J = 860 kcal
1 Btu = 1.056×10^3 J

Power

1 W = 1 J/s = 0.7376 ft·lb/s = 3.41 Btu/h
1 hp = 550 ft·lb/s = 746 W

Pressure

1 atm = 1.01325 bar = 1.01325×10^5 N/m^2
     = 14.7 lb/in.^{2} = 760 torr
1 lb/in.^{2} = 6.895×10^3 N/m^2
1 Pa = 1 N/m^2 = 1.450×10^{-4} lb/in.^{2}

SI Derived Units and Their Abbreviations

Quantity	Unit	Abbreviation	In Terms of Base Units†
Force	newton	N	kg·m/s^2
Energy and work	joule	J	kg·m^2/s^2
Power	watt	W	kg·m^2/s^3
Pressure	pascal	Pa	kg/(m·s^2)
Frequency	hertz	Hz	s^{-1}
Electric charge	coulomb	C	A·s
Electric potential	volt	V	kg·m^2/(A·s^3)
Electric resistance	ohm	Ω	kg·m^2/(A^2·s^3)
Capacitance	farad	F	A^2·s^4/(kg·m^2)
Magnetic field	tesla	T	kg/(A·s^2)
Magnetic flux	weber	Wb	kg·m^2/(A·s^2)
Inductance	henry	H	kg·m^2/(A^2·s^2)

†kg = kilogram (mass), m = meter (length), s = second (time), A = ampere (electric current).

Metric (SI) Multipliers

Prefix	Abbreviation	Value
yotta	Y	10^{24}
zeta	Z	10^{21}
exa	E	10^{18}
peta	P	10^{15}
tera	T	10^{12}
giga	G	10^9
mega	M	10^6
kilo	k	10^3
hecto	h	10^2
deka	da	10^1
deci	d	10^{-1}
centi	c	10^{-2}
milli	m	10^{-3}
micro	μ	10^{-6}
nano	n	10^{-9}
pico	p	10^{-12}
femto	f	10^{-15}
atto	a	10^{-18}
zepto	z	10^{-21}
yocto	y	10^{-24}